The
Inventor's
Handbook

Canadian representatives: General Publishing Co., Ltd., 30 Lesmill Road, Don Mills, Ontario M3B 2T6.

9 8 7 6
Digit on the right indicates the number of this printing.

Library of Congress Cataloging-in-Publication Number 93–87586

ISBN 1–56138–459–3

Package and book cover design by Toby Schmidt.
Package illustration by Jon Pochos.
Package photography by Steve Mullen.
Book interior design by Paul Kepple.
Book interior illustration by Julie Fraenkel.
Edited by David Borgenicht.
Typography: Bembo and Copperplate by Deborah Lugar.
Museum of Science Product Development Staff: Jen Lisle, Ric Craig.

A Note to Parents:

This interactive, educational kit is designed to teach and entertain children, but it contains small parts which could cause injury, including severe injury if swallowed or used near the eyes. This kit should not be used by children under four years of age without adult supervision. Please read the complete instructions inside before using this kit.

This book may be ordered by mail from the publisher.
Please add $2.50 for postage and handling.
But try your bookstore first!

Running Press Book Publishers
125 South Twenty-second Street
Philadelphia, Pennsylvania 19103–4399

BOSTON'S MUSEUM OF SCIENCE

THE
INVENTOR'S
HANDBOOK

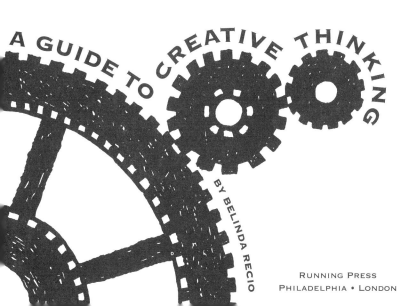

A GUIDE TO CREATIVE THINKING

BY BELINDA RECIO

RUNNING PRESS
PHILADELPHIA • LONDON

CONTENTS

PART ONE:

PART TWO:

PART THREE:

PART FOUR:

PART FIVE:

WHAT IS AN INVENTION?

An invention is something new created by a human being. Many inventions result from bringing together existing materials and technologies in a new way. Often, inventions are a response to a specific human need or desire—a faster way to connect different parts of clothing (the zipper), a device to wipe the water off a windshield (windshield wipers), or a way to eat meat without getting your hands dirty (the sandwich).

Many people think of creation, discovery, and design as invention. There's no doubt that these activities have things in common—all of them require the ability to visualize lots of possibilities. However, there are some differences.

A creation is usually created for its own sake—such as art or music.

A discovery, unlike an invention, exists *before* it is found (such as the discovery of America, electricity, and the latex sap of the rubber tree). Many discoveries often lead to inventions. For example, scientists discovered that the extract from willow tree bark was a pain reliever, but they also found that it caused stomach disorders. Eventually, a chemist made a synthetic version of the chemical found in the extract. This new invention, called aspirin, does not usually cause stomach disorders.

Design is different from both creation and invention; it doesn't usually involve making new things. Design involves changing, or adapting, things that already exist. For example, an automotive designer might come up with a new design for a car, but this new design relies on basic automobile structure. The new car would still have wheels, an engine, a transmission, a body, and so forth. An inventor, on the other hand, might invent a whole new type of car—perhaps one that doesn't have wheels!

Invention usually begins with *need*—and that need often becomes *want*. Think about a knife; it was invented by Stone Age people who needed to cut up food.

Now think about a complicated food processor used to quickly cut, slice, and process everything from carrots to beef. We do not need food processors in order to cook and eat. However, many people want food processors because they save time, and often do a better job than a knife.

An old saying claims that "necessity is the mother of invention." It may be that in reality, necessity *and* desire are its parents.

HOW TO USE THIS KIT

This book is your guide to inventive thinking and invention-making. It's divided into five parts.

This section, part one, helps to get you started by introducing you to inventive thinking, both creative and critical.

The next part is a workshop that introduces you to the materials in this kit, and their many uses. You can apply what you learn in this section to your inventions.

Part three is where you can become an inventor. It consists of five *Invention Challenges*, each one a test of what you've learned and how inventively you can think. Each one begins with an introduction to related inventions and scientific principles. The five challenges are not instructions for making inventions, but rather a set of guidelines that will help you to think inventively as you solve the challenge.

"If You Get Stuck" follows the challenges. This section isn't an answer key; there aren't any "right answers." The solutions are included in case you have a tough time with a particular challenge and need a shortcut. (Don't worry if you do get stuck—inventors often have to rethink their original ideas.)

Finally, part five tells you how to patent your ideas to protect your inventions. Let's start inventing!

YOUNG INVENTOR PROFILE

Chester Greenwood was 15 years old when he invented earmuffs. He thought of the idea while skating outdoors in Maine—to protect his ears, he tied a wool scarf around his head.

The scarf was warm, but the wool was itchy, so he tried another idea. He bent wire into two loops and asked his grandmother to sew fur and velvet around the loops. She used another piece of wire to connect the loops to each other and sewed the wire into his hat.

These innovative earmuffs kept Chester warm, and soon, others were asking for them. Over the next few years, Chester continued to improve his invention. He obtained a patent in 1877, when he was 19.

Although the invention was named Greenwood's Ear Protectors, they are still commonly known as earmuffs.

THINK ABOUT THINKING

People don't usually think about thinking. After all, thinking comes naturally to us, so why think about it? Because if you think about how you think, you can learn to think inventively.

Inventive thinking is an attitude—a special way of thinking. It says, "Will it work? Let's try it and find out!"

There's always more than one way to think about things. If you're having a hard time solving a problem—whether it's making an invention or doing a project for school—it may be because you're fixed on doing something in only one way. Some people describe this as having a mental block, or tunnel vision.

We frequently see what we expect to see. But if you can learn to look carefully at the world around you, without tunnel vision, you'll probably see a lot of things that other people miss. Something that only you see could lead to a new idea for a great invention!

When you think inventively, you try to see beyond your mental blocks by asking yourself questions such as: How else might I think about this? How else could this be used? Could it work another way?

Those questions are examples of the thinking tools that can help you to think inventively and become an inventor.

GATHERING YOUR THINKING TOOLS

The most important tools in your inventor's workshop are not the materials included in this kit. The most important tools are your *thinking tools*—questions that you ask yourself so that you can keep an open mind and think inventively. They're strategies or rules of thumb for generating ideas and solving problems.

There are two types of thinking tools—creative tools (that help you imagine possibilities) and critical tools (that help you compare, contrast, and analyze).

Here are typical questions that you should ask yourself at each stage of your invention:

Questions for Creative Thinking

1. What else might work? What other choices are there?
2. What other things might this be used for?
3. What could I add?
4. What could I subtract?
5. How could it be rearranged?
6. What parts could I substitute for other parts?
7. What parts could I combine?
8. What's the opposite of this invention?
9. Could this invention be made smaller or larger?

Questions for Critical Thinking

1. Is it safe?

2. Is it practical?

3. Is it as simple as it can be?

4. Will it cost too much to make?

5. Do I have the tools and materials I need to make it?

6. Can I make it easily?

7. Is it worth making?

8. Should it be redesigned?

You can turn back to this section when you read "Part Three: The Invention Challenges" to help you crystallize your thinking.

OTHER THINKING TOOLS

If you can see something in your mind, you can *visualize* it. Practice trying to see your ideas in your head, and once you can see them draw a sketch. Then ask yourself if you can see it a different way.

Another helpful skill is doing something without preparation or practice. This is called *improvising*. Usually preparation helps, but sometimes it can make you develop tunnel vision. When this happens, improvise! Try something new that you didn't plan on doing.

Failure is also important, although it doesn't always seem that way. When you set out to invent something and fail, your failure demands that you use all your thinking tools to figure out how to try it again. As you work through the cycle of trial and error, you learn valuable information about what does and doesn't work. So don't be afraid to fail!

On the other hand, if you get it right the first time, chances are that you won't learn as much—or that your goal was too easy. Whenever you try something and get it right the first time, try it again, but make it more challenging the second time around.

THE LIMITATIONS OF LOGIC

Logic can be a great tool, but it can also cause you to have tunnel vision and only see things that "make sense." Many things would never have been invented or discovered if people always followed the straight and narrow path of logic.

When Luigi Galvani was studying frog anatomy in 1786, he used two metal rods to examine a frog. At one point, the frog's leg twitched! Galvani thought that the frog's body had electricity in it. After all, it was the frog's body that had twitched, so this was the "logical" conclusion.

Later, another scientist, Alessandro Volta, figured out that the metal rods had caused the electricity, not the frog itself. He used his discovery to invent the first battery, which was simply an acid-soaked pad placed between two metal rods.

The real reason why the frog's leg twitched did not seem logical—after all, if the frog's body had twitched, it must have been caused by something within the frog's body. But eventually, they discovered that the illogical conclusion was in fact the true conclusion.

The moral is: Use logic when it works for you, but if you have an illogical idea, go for it!

YOUNG INVENTOR PROFILE

Second grader Eric Vendura invented a Sleeve Stopper, a loop of elastic that attaches to a shirt or sweater sleeve. You hook your thumb in the loop before putting on your coat, and your sleeves won't bunch up.

THE WORKSHOP

PART TWO

Meet Your Materials

The materials in this kit have been selected because each one has many uses. This section presents a few of the uses for each of the components—uses you will need to know when you get down to inventing.

Try the uses as they are presented to you. This will help you to understand the materials better and to apply what you learn to your inventions.

Don't limit yourself to the uses presented here. There are probably hundreds—even thousands—of other uses.

Things to Use from Your Home

The invention challenges will require materials in addition to those included in this kit. The other materials that you'll need aren't unusual or hard-to-find—they're common household items. Below is a list of helpful materials that you might find use for in your Inventor's Workshop.

Don't bother about collecting all of this now—just keep your eyes out for these helpful materials as you think inventively.

An Inventor's Notebook

A blank notebook for your ideas and sketches

Kitchen Materials

milk cartons

tin cans

lids

plastic sandwich bags

plastic wrap

wax paper

aluminum foil

paper bags

paper plates

plastic or styrofoam cups

paper towel tubes

foil pie pans

plastic bag twist-ties

toothpicks

Popsicle sticks

plastic or paper straws

Craft Materials

yarn

film canisters

balloons

magnets

scraps of fabric

buttons

clothespins

marbles

modeling clay

broken toys

Office or Desk Materials

paper clips

rubber bands

safety pins

glue

ball-point pens

cardboard

tape

string

tacks

pins

rulers

empty boxes

coat hangers

Hardware Materials

nails

metal washers

scrap lumber and plastic

tubing (plastic or rubber)

pulleys

hooks

nuts and bolts

screws

wire

springs

flashlight batteries and bulbs

wheels

fishing line

Bathroom Materials

toilet paper tubes

petroleum jelly

INVENTING WITH WOODEN SPOOLS

Wooden spools: four

The wooden spool probably evolved from the spindle, which is a part of a spinning wheel. A spindle is a rod that holds a spool-like device, onto which thread is wound. The spindle was most likely invented by women as long ago as 6500 B.C.

As you can imagine, spools can be used in hundreds of ways. Here are a few ideas to help your brainstorming.

Wheels for Vehicles. One of the most important mechanical inventions of all time, the wheel is found

on all sorts of machines. The first wheel appeared in ancient Meso-
potamia, more than 5,000 years ago. Wheels revolutionized transportation,
making it possible to move faster and more materials than ever before.

Wheel-and-Axle Machines. A wheel-and-axle machine
is used to transmit force. It acts as a lever that rotates around
a fixed point.

The steering wheel of a car and the handle of a screw-
driver are wheel-and-axle machines because they increase
the force of your hands as you turn them.

Windlasses. The windlass is another ancient device used
to lift objects. The windlass is similar to the pulley on the
next page, except that it winds the cord *onto* the wheel,
instead of pulling the cord over it. This is a type of wheel-
and-axle machine because it uses a hand crank. An
example is the crank that raises and lowers the bucket in a well. The hand
crank transmits and increases the force of your arm to the wheel that raises
and lowers the bucket.

Spool Motors. Many motors work by spinning—the spin
produces energy. You can make a spool motor with a rubber
band and a few other materials. For complete instructions on
how to create a spool motor, see "Rubber–Band Motors" on
pages 23–24.

Pulley Systems. The pulley has been around for thousands of years. It's one of the most useful lifting devices, because pulling down is easier than pulling up—and that's what pulleys are all about.

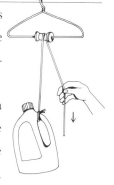

A pulley is simply a wheel attached to a support and a cord. The cord runs over the wheel and is attached to the object you wish to lift (called the load). When you pull the cord down, the load is lifted up. Thus, when you use a pulley, the weight of your body works for you, not against you.

Block and Tackle Systems. Add another wheel to the pulley and you've created a block and tackle, a device used to make lifting heavy objects easier. Try lifting an object with a single pulley.

Now add another pulley as shown above, and try lifting the same object. It should be much easier! To make it even easier to lift, add a weight to the end you pull on. Now the slightest tug should raise the load.

Bases and Connectors. A wooden spool can be used as a base that supports a structure, or as a cuff to connect two things.

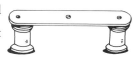

Use it as the bottom of a tower or another structure, or stick dowels in the holes to hold them together.

INVENTING WITH RUBBER BANDS

Rubber bands: three

The ancient Mayans were the first to use rubber. They made rubber shoes by dipping their feet in latex, the milky sap of the rubber tree, and letting them dry. Much later, in 1820, an Englishman named Thomas Hancock sliced a rubber bottle into rings and used these rings for garters and waistbands. Hancock never patented his unique invention.

Twenty-five years later, in 1845, another Englishman named Stephen Perry opened up a rubber-band factory and patented the rubber band.

There are three rubber bands in this kit, one long and two short ones. The following examples should help you jump-start your own brainstorming about the uses of rubber bands.

Fasteners. Rubber bands are most often used as fasteners. They're ideal for holding things together. Don't overlook this simple function as you make your own inventions!

Rubber-Band Motors. Energy produced by motion is called kinetic energy. Some motors—including rubber-band motors—produce a type of kinetic energy called mechanical energy.

To make a rubber-band motor, insert a rubber band through the hole of a spool. The rubber band should be only slightly longer than the spool. Place a washer (metal or homemade) at one end and slip a toothpick through the loop of rubber band that sticks out from the washer. Slip a toothpick through the rubber band at the other end of the spool and tape it to the spool.

Now rotate the toothpick at the washer end of the spool to wind up the rubber band. When you release the toothpick, the rubber band will quickly unwind, producing mechanical energy that can be used to power many different types of inventions!

Slingshots and Launching Devices. The elasticity of a rubber band makes it ideal for launching or propelling objects.

When you stretch a rubber band, it has *stored energy*. When you release the most tightly stretched side, it snaps back with enough force to move an object such as a marble or a paper airplane into the air or along a surface.

Can you figure out how a stretched and twisted rubber band can be used to make an object spin?

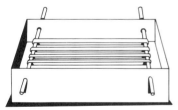

Sound Makers. Rubber bands can produce a variety of sounds. If several rubber bands are stretched to different lengths and then plucked, different pitches and tones will come out. Each band will vibrate according to how tightly it is stretched. Different vibrations produce different air waves, which result in different sounds.

How does varying the length or width of the rubber bands change the sounds they make?

Belt Systems. Belts can be used to connect wheels and gears, which transfer motion, energy, and force in a machine.

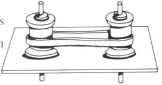

A belt stretched between two gears or two freely rotating wheels—perhaps even two spools—allows one wheel to move the other wheel. If you twist a rubber band in a figure eight before looping it over the wheels, the motion of one wheel causes the other wheel to move in the opposite direction.

Tread. Rubber bands can be used as tread to give traction to a spool wheel.

Inventing with Marbles

Marbles: two

Marbles made of baked clay have been found in prehistoric archaeological sites, and the ancient Romans played games with marbles more than two thousand years ago!

Here are some of the many uses for marbles.

Ball Bearings. Ball bearings make things easier to move by changing sliding motion into rolling motion. This reduces friction and increases movement.

Here's how to use ball bearings to move things. Create a

straight track by lining up two long dowels so that they're parallel. Or, create a circular track by using the top of a can.

Place several marbles inside the track (use extras from around your home if you need to). Now, position the object you want to move—try a book—on top of the marbles. Give the book a spin or a push, and see how it moves.

Pendulums. A marble can be used as a pendulum. Wrap a small rubber band around the marble to create a net-like effect.

Now tie a piece of string to the rubber band. Hang the marble pendulum from a dowel and start it swinging back and forth!

Energy Transporters. Marbles can be put to work to transfer energy.

To demonstrate, create a straight track with several dowels, or use the edges of books. Lift one end to create a short ramp. Place one marble near the end of the track, and release the other one from the top of the ramp.

When it hits the stationary marble, that marble moves. This is called energy transfer. Now try this with two marbles on the track. What happens?

You can use the marble to move other materials.

Inventing with Dowels

Dowels: two

A dowel is a peg made of wood or another material. It's usually used to hold two things together. People have been using wooden pegs to hold things together ever since they discovered ways to shape and cut wood into functional tools and objects.

Structural Supports. Dowels can be used to add strength and form to an object, much like a skeleton does in our bodies. A sail, for example, needs a center support beam. A tipi is made by securing hides to several support poles.

Levers. A lever is a stiff bar or pole that balances on or turns around a fixed support called a *fulcrum*.

A seesaw is a good example of a lever. When force is applied at one end of the pole, the other end is raised in the air. The nearer a heavy object is to the fulcrum, the less energy it takes to lift it.

Axles. Dowels can be used as axles in many kinds of inventions. You can make a wheel-and-axle machine using a spool for a wheel and a dowel for an axle. You can use the dowels as axles for wheels on a vehicle.

Shafts. A dowel can also serve as a shaft or rod. A pulley system usually needs to be suspended from a strong shaft.

A dowel can be used as the shaft of a pinwheel or propeller.

Conveyors. A conveyor moves objects from one place to another. Although a conveyor usually uses a belt to move objects, it can also use dowels.

Punch holes evenly along two long sides of a thin box. Insert the dowels so that they spin freely in the holes. You've made a simple conveyor!

INVENTING WITH GEARS

Gears: three

Pointer and handle: one

Gears are wheels with teeth. They interlock and move one another to transmit energy and force that are used to do mechanical work.

Gears are some of the oldest mechanical devices. They were used by the ancient Egyptians, Greeks, and Romans.

Speed Shifters. Gears are often used to change the speed of a machine. 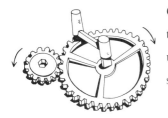 Gears of different sizes are combined in different ways to accomplish this goal. For instance, motion is sped up if a large gear turns a smaller gear and slowed if a small gear turns a larger one.

Power Increasers. Different-size gears connected in a series can increase the force produced by a machine.

Examples of machines that use gears are a ten-speed bicycle, a manual eggbeater, a clock, and a water wheel.

INVENTING WITH DRILLED SPLINTS

Drilled splints: six

The splints included in this kit look like the tongue depressors used by doctors to examine our throats. They also look like the supports you find inside popsicles and other food products.

Structural Supports. Splints make excellent support beams and frames for your inventions. You can create structures and frames by placing dowels through the holes in the splints, and by connecting them with rubber bands, tacks, or tape. Use them to build the frames of cars, airplanes, boats, or rockets. Build a frame to mount the motor in this kit, or to support a pulley or gear system. Hang things from them to make a mobile.

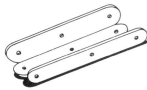

Tracks and Channels. Use the splints to make tracks or channels on which to roll marbles or vehicles.

Ramps and Springboards. Use the splints as ramps to roll or slide things up or down on, or as springboards to bounce things.

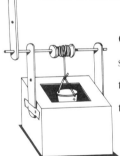

Paddles and Blades. Fans, propellers, windmills, water wheels, and paddle boats all use paddles or blades as surfaces to push against water or air.

Splints can act as these paddles and blades. Will the holes in the splints be a problem? If so, how can you solve this problem?

Levers. Place a splint over a fulcrum to make a lever to lift or to balance objects.

Crank Arms. You can use a splint as a crank arm on a gear system or in a windlass. To make the crank, attach the splint to a moving part of your invention, such as a gear or wheel, that you need to rotate or crank.

INVENTING WITH A MOTOR

Motor: one

Warning: Never immerse a motor or batteries in water!

A motor is a machine that turns electrical energy into mechanical energy. The development of electric motors began in the 1800s with the discovery of the electromagnet.

You'll need a battery to power the motor. Batteries come in different strengths, and the strength of the battery will affect the speed of the motor. Some of your inventions may require greater speed and strength than others, so experiment.

There are other motor principles with which you might want to experiment. For instance, what happens if you attach the wires to the battery poles, and then reverse them?

There is one electric motor in this kit, with two wires attached to it. To turn it on, you'll need to connect the motor to a battery by attaching one wire to each battery end. You may need to strip the plastic coating off the wire to make the connection. You can use a small pair of scissors or wire strippers to do this. (You can also make a switch to turn your motor on and off by breaking the circuit. See "Switches" on page 36 for complete instructions.)

Power Source. You can use the motor in this kit to power a wheeled vehicle.

Try constructing a treaded vehicle—like a tank—using rubber bands stretched between spools. Use the motor to move parts of other inventions.

Miniature Fan. If you attach the propeller from the kit to the motor's shaft, you'll have a miniature fan, or perhaps another source of power for a vehicle.

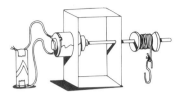

Motorized Lifting Device. To make a motorized lifting system, attach the motor to a windlass or pulley.

INVENTING WITH A PROPELLER

Propeller: one

A propeller is a device consisting of radiating blades, attached to the center of a revolving shaft. Airplane propellers are also known as air screws.

The first successful propeller with blades was developed in 1836 by John Ericsson, a Swedish-American inventor. Ericsson also introduced propellers on ships as engines. And in 1903, the Wright brothers built and flew the first successful airplane, which had two propellers located behind the wings.

The propeller in this kit has two blades and a hole in the center so that you can attach it to a shaft. The shaft on the end of the electric motor fits inside this hole.

Power Source. Attached to a rubber band-spool motor or an electric motor, a propeller spins and pushes out the air in the direction of its spin. This pushed air (called *thrust*) can provide energy to power a vehicle.

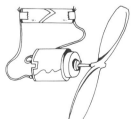

Fan. You can attach the propeller to a motor and use it to push air out, which can cool objects or people.

Energy Transporter. You can use the thrust produced by a motorized propeller to move an object. Try setting up a transfer of energy "system" in which you use the thrust from the propeller somewhere along the path.

For instance, you might begin by rolling a marble down a ramp so that it hits a lever, which then moves a sail (a piece of paper attached to a dowel) in the line of thrust from the propeller. The thrust would cause the sail to spin, which in turn could transfer energy to the next step in your transfer of energy system.

INVENTING WITH A BELL

Bell: one

A bell is a hollow vessel, usually made of metal, with a clapper or a tongue inside. When the bell is moved or shaken, the clapper hits the sides of the vessel, causing it to ring.

The bell was born in Asia, where it was used in ceremonies. In ancient Greece, a bell might have announced the arrival of a fresh catch of fish at the market, or warned of an approaching enemy. In Rome and around the world today, bells still call people to religious services and remind students that they have to get to class.

Music Maker. Attach the bell to a rotating spool, spinning propeller, or a splint that you can shake to make jingle music.

Time Marker. If you invent a machine that makes repetitive motions or revolutions, use the bell to mark the interval of one complete motion (or the end of a task). Many timers do this.

For instance, make an arm that will strike the bell when a gear or water wheel has made one complete turn.

Alarm. Use the bell to alert yourself or others of the presence of something or someone. You might attach the bell to a door so that you know when someone opens it.

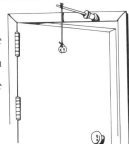

Location Tracker. Use the bell on a self-propelled vehicle to track its position. The sound of the bell will help you to locate it.

INVENTING WITH A STRAW

Straw: one

Marvin Chester Stone made the first artificial straw in 1886. It was made of waxed Manila paper and hand rolled. Straws were handmade until 1905, when the first straw-making machine was invented by the M.C.S. Estate.

Arms and Tubes. You can use a straw for the arms of a mobile, the spokes of a wheel, or wherever you need a flexible, bendable tube.

Air or Water Pipe. Air directed down a tube is compressed and gains power and force, especially when it escapes and expands out the other end of the tube. Use a straw with balloons and propellers to make jets, cars, rockets, or boats.

You can use the same principle to force water through a tube.

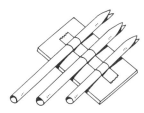

Sound Maker. Several lengths of straw can be put together to make a Pan flute.

To make a Pan flute, cut the straws into different sizes and tape them together, from longest to shortest. When you blow over the ends, they will vibrate and create sounds. The longer the straw, the lower the sound it produces.

Blow the flute into a tin can to make different sounds. The vibration of the tin—called resonance—changes the sounds produced by the flute.

Connector. A straw can be used to connect two dowels, or to extend their length. Slip a dowel in each end of a straw and secure them with tape. The straw adds flexibility to the rigid dowels, allowing you to bend around corners.

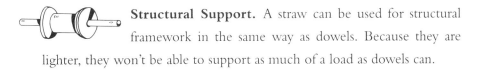

Structural Support. A straw can be used for structural framework in the same way as dowels. Because they are lighter, they won't be able to support as much of a load as dowels can.

On the other hand, their light weight makes them better suited for inventions that need to be light, such as flying inventions.

INVENTING WITH BRASS FASTENERS

Brass fasteners: eight

A brass fastener is a small connecting device, used to hold objects together. Fasteners are usually used for papers, but they can also connect other light materials—for example, drilled splints.

Connectors. You can insert a brass fastener through two materials (such as the holes in two splints) and bend back the two ends of the fastener. The two materials are now attached.

Notice that one of the "legs" has a pointed end. You can use this pointed end to press through soft materials, such as paper and fabric.

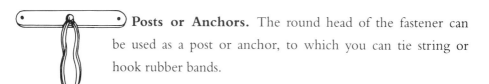

Posts or Anchors. The round head of the fastener can be used as a post or anchor, to which you can tie string or hook rubber bands.

Switches. Brass fasteners can be used to build a switch to turn motors on and off. A switch makes or breaks a circuit, which is a combination of electrically-connected things, like a motor, a battery, and wire.

To make a simple switch for the motor, you'll need two brass fasteners, a paper clip, a small piece of cardboard, wire, a battery, and the motor.

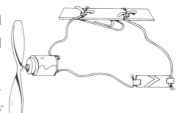

Push one brass fastener through the cardboard. Slip a paper clip around the head of the brass fastener. Push another brass fastener through the cardboard. Position it close to the other one so that the other end of the paper clip can touch it.

Wrap one of the motor's wires around the legs of a brass fastener. Tape the other motor wire to one end of a battery. Now take a third piece of wire and tape one end to the opposite end of the battery, and the other end to the legs of the second brass fastener.

To turn the switch on, move the paper clip so that it touches both brass fasteners. To turn it off, swing the paper clip away from one brass fastener.

YOUNG INVENTOR PROFILE

Akhil Rastogi was 7 years old when he invented the E-Z Gallon, a spill proof bottle spout that makes it easier to pour large containers of milk or juice.

When he had achieved a successful design, Akhil approached the U.S. Patent Office. It turned out that he had designed something new, and after two years of work, he was awarded a patent for his E-Z Gallon in 1992.

THE INVENTION CHALLENGES

Before You Invent

Some materials in this kit can be used and reused with very little alteration. For instance, you might use the spools as wheels for a vehicle, and then take apart the vehicle and use the spools for a pulley system.

Chances are that you'll do no damage to the spools when you use them as wheels, so they'll be in fine condition to use for a pulley system, or another purpose.

But other materials in this kit *cannot* be used more than once if they are used in certain ways, so they require a little more planning if you want to be able to reuse them. You cannot, for example, cut a straw and then expect to "put it back together." So try to plan ahead as you use the materials.

Think of the materials in this kit as the beginnings of your Inventor's Workshop. If you collect other common materials, you won't have to worry about using up the kit—because you'll have a collection of many things to use!

About the Invention Challenges

The Invention Challenges aren't step-by-step instructions. They're a set of guidelines and questions to help you think inventively and to create your *own* devices, not recreate other people's ideas.

Each challenge begins with an introduction that has helpful information about related inventions and scientific principles. The introduction, like the section about the materials, is important to your training as an inventor. As you read it, you can think about how to apply the information to your invention ideas.

BACK TO THE DRAWING BOARD

After you've completed your invention, try to improve it by redesigning it on paper.

When you invent on paper, it isn't necessary to have all of the required materials. All you need is the experience you just gained from making the first version of the invention and your imagination.

Remember, when you go back to the drawing board, the sky's the limit!

INVENTION CHALLENGE #1:
INVENT A TIME TRACKER

All timekeeping devices, from a simple shadow clock to a precision Swiss watch, have one thing in common: they track the passage of time by repeatedly performing an action that can be measured.

A sundial casts a shadow that moves across its face. A water clock drips water until it is empty. A pendulum clock tracks the swinging of a pendulum. What will yours do?

Shadow Clocks. One of the oldest forms of time-tracking devices is the sundial.

You tell time with a sundial by watching the movement of the shadow cast by the sundial's centerpiece, called a *gnomen*. This centerpiece can be a simple stick secured in the ground, or a more elaborate vertical object attached to the face of a sundial. The length of the shadow cast by the gnomen corresponds to the sun's position overhead. As the sun moves across the sky, the shadow of the gnomen moves across the face of the sundial. (The shortest shadow always occurs at 12 noon, when the sun is at its highest point in the sky.)

Water Clocks. Ancient water clocks tracked time by regulating the flow of water through a hole. In early clocks, a piece of pottery was marked with lines and filled to the top with water. Then a tiny hole in the bottom was unplugged.

The water dripped out at a regular rate, marking a segment of time as each line was revealed by the falling water level.

Some water clocks operated by filling a vessel with water rather than emptying one. In this case, as each line was covered with water, a segment of time was marked.

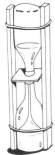

Sand Clocks. The most common sand clock is the hourglass. This is a glass cylinder with a pinched middle through which grains of sand fall at a regular rate.

When all of the sand flows to the bottom of the cylinder, one hour has passed. You measure the next hour by turning over the hourglass to start the sand flowing again.

The Pendulum Clock. Galileo first noticed the regularity of a swinging object in the 1580s. He was watching the chandelier that hung from the ceiling of his church swing back and forth. He timed the swinging by using his pulse rate to keep track of the motion. After watching for several minutes, he found that the swinging stayed regular—it didn't slow down or speed up. Galileo thought that this swinging motion could be used to make a clock.

Although he never made a pendulum clock, several centuries later in 1657, the Dutch scientist Christian Huygens did. Pendulums were eventually combined with wheels, gears, and springs to move the hands on a clock face.

The pendulum can still be seen today in many grandfather clocks, swinging back and forth and creating the familiar "tick-tock."

Gears and Clocks. Gears come in many different sizes and can be combined with weights, springs, belts, and pendulums to control the rate and direction of motion.

If you could see the inside of a wind-up watch, you'd see a collection of interlocking gears attached to the winding spring and the hands of the watch. The gears act as transformers of energy and motion.

THE CHALLENGE

Now that you've learned about timekeeping devices throughout history, you can invent one of your own. Use any or all of the materials in this kit, as well as any household tools and materials that you have collected.

The only requirement is that the Time Tracker must mark the passage of time. How it tracks time, and how much time it tracks, is up to you.

⚙ STEP ONE: BRAINSTORM

List, sketch, and discuss your ideas for a time tracker. Don't limit yourself to just a few ideas and don't force yourself to think of dozens. When you've listed all of your ideas, you're ready to move on.

⚙ STEP TWO: ASK QUESTIONS AND THINK INVENTIVELY

Now challenge your brain to use what it knows. Turn back to review the "Meet Your Materials" section, and the descriptions of time tracking machines if you need to.

Here are some questions to help you imagine and analyze your invention ideas.

Questions and Ideas for Creative Thinking:

The sun moves, water drips, sand drops, and a pendulum swings. These are some of the things that can be measured and used to track the passage of time.

What other things can be measured and used to track time?

What do sand and water have in common? Are there other things like sand and water that you can use?

What about the earth's movement around the sun—are there other things that appear to move across the sky that you can use to track time?

What about connecting the movement of water or sand to something else that is connected to a pointer, like the hands of a clock?

Questions and Ideas for Critical Thinking:

List the timekeeping devices presented on the previous pages and rate them according to effectiveness and limitations. For example, how is a sundial limited? Are there places you can't use it? Are there certain times of day when it wouldn't work? Is it affected by the weather?

What about the water clock—how is it limited? Would temperature affect it? How?

What other limitations do your ideas have? What advantages?

How long a period of time would you like your invention to track?

⚙ STEP THREE: INVENT IT

The invention must be yours, so now you're on your own. Remember, there are hundreds of ways to invent any one device—there's no one correct answer. Use all that you have learned to try your invention—and most importantly, if it doesn't work, keep on trying. Go back to the "Thinking Tools" section and Step Two to figure out where you went wrong.

If you get stuck and need a hint, turn to "If You Get Stuck" on page 65. And if you really need help, look at the solution in the same section for one possible inventive answer.

What are you waiting for? Be inventive!

INVENTION CHALLENGE #2: INVENT A FLYING MACHINE

People have been fascinated by flight since the beginning of recorded history. In fact, the ancient Greek myth of Daedalus is about a man who straps on a set of wings in order to escape his captors.

In the 1500s, Leonardo da Vinci, the famous artist and inventor, drew pictures of a "flapping wing machine." But it wasn't Leonardo's invention that first delivered human beings to the skies. It was much later, in 1783, that people first experienced flight—in a hot-air balloon.

The Hot-Air Balloon. When people stopped studying birds and started to study what the birds fly through—the air—they learned the secret of flight! Air is a real substance—it's a mixture of gasses, and it has certain properties, including weight.

So, when scientists first started to experiment with air to learn the secret of flight, they began by trying to make objects lighter than air.

They first tried to remove the air from inside the objects they wanted to fly. Although this didn't work, they were on the right track. In the 1700s, two Frenchmen filled a silk bag with smoke. They noticed that smoke rises and thought that they could make something fly if they filled it with smoke. Indeed, the bag rose right to the ceiling!

It was later discovered that it was the hot air and not the smoke itself that made the bag rise.

Parachutes. Parachutes don't fly up, but they fall so slowly through the air that they are used to deliver people safely to the ground. The reason for the slow descent of a parachute is *air resistance*.

Parachutes rely on air that flows in the opposite direction of their descent, called *drag*. Drag can be used to slow things down, and it's one of the forces that affect flight.

Wings and Daniel Bernoulli. Daniel Bernoulli (1700-1782) was a Swiss scientist who studied the behavior of gasses and fluids. (A fluid, not to be confused with a liquid, is anything that flows, including air and water.) Bernoulli discovered an extremely important principle: fast-moving air exerts less pressure than slow-moving air.

Taking this principle one step further, he pointed out that when air travels over curved surfaces, it has further to go than when it travels over straight surfaces—so it travels faster.

This is why airplane wings are curved on top and straighter on the bottom. The air moves faster over the top, curved surface of the wing. This fast-moving air exerts less pressure than the slow-moving air underneath the wing, so the wing is lifted up by the air pressure underneath it.

Jets, Rockets, and Sir Isaac Newton. Jets and rockets are called reaction vehicles because they are perfect examples of Newton's third law of motion: "For every action there is an equal and opposite reaction." Think about it as an equation: for every backward push there is a forward movement.

For rockets, this means that when the hot gasses produced in the engine expand and rush out the exhaust, rockets move forward—action and reaction. A jet engine works by sucking air in at the front end of the jet and ejecting it at very high speeds at the back of the jet. The jet moves forward as the air streams backward.

THE CHALLENGE

Now that you've learned a few of the principles of aerodynamics, you can invent your own flying machine. Use any or all of the materials in this kit, as well as any household tools and materials that you may have collected.

The flying machine must fly. How high or far it flies, and which principles it uses to fly, is up to you.

✹ STEP ONE: BRAINSTORM

List, sketch, and discuss your ideas for a flying machine. Don't limit yourself to just a few ideas or force yourself to think of too many. When you've finished brainstorming, gather your thoughts and ideas, and move on.

✹ STEP TWO: ASK QUESTIONS AND THINK INVENTIVELY

Now challenge your brain again. Here are questions for you to consider.

Questions and Ideas for Creative Thinking:

Hot air rises, drag slows things down, fast-moving air has less pressure than slow-moving air, and for every action there is an equal and opposite reaction. These principles can be applied to making things that stay aloft in the air and fly.

What other things should you consider when inventing a flying machine?

How will the shape of your flying machine affect its flight? What sort of shape do planes, jets, and rockets have?

How is shape related to drag?

What materials would work best for a flying machine?

Questions and Ideas for Critical Thinking:

How can you redesign your flying machine so that it flies faster?

What can you change about how it is launched? Is it launched by your arm or does it have another power source?

What else could you use as a power source?

How can you redesign your flying machine so that it stays in the air longer?

Does weight affect the amount of time it stays in the air? Does weight affect speed?

⚙ STEP THREE: INVENT IT!

Once again, you're on your own. Remember, that there's no one correct answer, so use all that you have learned to try your invention. If it doesn't work, keep on trying—go back to the "Thinking Tools" section and Step Two to figure out where you went wrong.

If you get stuck and need a hint, turn to "If You Get Stuck" on page 65. And if you really need help, look at the solution in the same section for one possible inventive answer.

INVENTION CHALLENGE #3: INVENT A SELF-PROPELLED VEHICLE

Over the centuries, people have invented many types of self-propelled vehicles. In the 1400s, windmill sails powered wooden carts. In the 1500s, steam was harnessed to power a wooden tractor. However, it wasn't until the mid-1700s that the first automobile was designed and built by Frenchman Nicolas Joseph Cugnat.

Cugnat's steam-driven vehicle could travel two miles an hour and could carry up to four people. Automobiles have come a long way since then, but their basic mechanical framework still reflects the design of the early inventors.

The Engine. Some form of power must be used to propel a vehicle. Early inventors used wind and steam, but modern cars use gasoline or diesel fuel.

In modern engines, fuel mixes with air in the engine's carburetor, is squeezed into a cylinder and forced upward by the pistons, and then is ignited by the spark plugs. This process is repeated hundreds of times per minute to produce the energy needed to move the car.

Other types of power used to propel vehicles include electrical motors, powered by traditional batteries or solar cells, and mechanical power created from a variety of sources—including human beings (as on bicycles).

The Drive Shaft. The engine is connected to other parts of the car by a shaft or rod that runs the length of the car, the *drive shaft*.

In early cars, simple leather belts drove gears and pulleys connected to the engine and the wheels. By the 1900s, leather was replaced by metal chains, which in turn were replaced by metal shafts. Today, cars have sophisticated drive shafts that connect intricate gear and crank systems to the steering column and wheel axles.

Wheels and Wheel Axles. Vehicle wheels are attached to axles, which are connected to the drive shaft. Wheels and axles can be connected in various ways; for instance, power can be connected only to the rear wheels, or to both front and rear wheels at the same time.

Cars can have any number of wheels. Consider the three-wheeled dune buggy, or the 18-wheel tractor-trailer. Some wheels are covered with rubber tires, which come in many designs for various purposes; heavily treaded snow tires, for example, or extra-wide racing tires.

Wheels can also be connected to one another by treaded belts, as in military tanks.

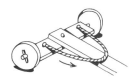

Steering Mechanisms. Every vehicle needs a way to control its direction. In cars, this is a steering column. At the top of the column is a large steering wheel. At the bottom, the steering column connects to the drive shaft, which can control the rear wheels, the front wheels, or both.

Thus, when the steering wheel is turned left, the wheels turn left, moving the car in that direction.

THE CHALLENGE

Now that you've learned about the basic parts of a self-propelled vehicle, it's time to invent a self-propelled vehicle of your own. Use any or all of the materials in this kit, as well as any household tools and materials that you may have collected.

The self-propelled vehicle must propel itself. How it propels itself, and how far it propels itself, is up to you.

✿ STEP ONE: BRAINSTORM

List, sketch, and discuss your ideas for a self-propelled vehicle. Don't limit yourself to just a few ideas or force yourself to think of dozens. When you have finished brainstorming, continue with Step Two.

✿ STEP TWO: ASK QUESTIONS AND THINK INVENTIVELY

You know that self-propelled vehicles need a source of power, a way to connect the power source to other parts of the car, and wheels.

Questions and Ideas for Creative Thinking:

Which materials in the kit could you use for wheels?

Do you have to use four wheels—or could you use an unusual number?

Will the wheels on your vehicle have any tread? What could you use for tread?

How will you connect the power source to the wheels?

What will you use for the vehicle's body or framework?

Can you combine materials to increase the vehicle's power?

What would happen if you combined the motor with the propeller?

Questions and Ideas for Critical Thinking:

Make a list of things you could use for a power source and then rate them according to how far and fast they could move a vehicle.

For example, after comparing the advantages and disadvantages of rubber-band and electric motors, you might conclude that the electric motor will last longer than the rubber-band motor—but you need a battery for the electric motor. And, the battery adds weight to the vehicle. Also, think about the position of the wheels, how they will affect the weight the vehicle can support, speed, and other factors.

Do the wheels need to lift the vehicle off the ground? What happens if the wheels do not lift the framework for the vehicle off the ground?

⚙ STEP THREE: INVENT IT!

Now, go to it. Use all that you have learned and always remember that there's no one answer. If your first invention doesn't work, keep on trying. Go back to the "Thinking Tools" section and Step Two if you need a refresher course.

If you get stuck and need a hint, turn to "If You Get Stuck" on page 65. And if you really need help, look at the solution in the same section for one possible inventive answer.

INVENTION CHALLENGE #4:
INVENT A MUSICAL THINGAMAGIG

A musical instrument is an object that produces sound in a rhythmic way. Fingers drumming on an empty soda can turn that can into a drum. In fact, drums originated in the ancient world's pots and pitchers.

The earliest instruments were objects found in nature—a conch shell that could be blown into like a horn, or a hollow log, for example. The first invented instruments were probably simple rhythm instruments, such as rattles. Next came percussion instruments, such as drums, and wind instruments, such as trumpets. String instruments such as the guitar, violin, and piano, came last.

There are four classes of instruments described below and a musical principle that will be helpful to you as you learn how instruments work.

 **String Instruments.** String instruments are played by either plucking or bowing strings. A guitar player plucks, whereas a violin player runs a bow over the strings. The tightness, looseness, and thickness of the strings affect the sound produced by the instrument.

Wind Instruments. Wind instruments are divided into two groups: woodwind and brass. Woodwinds use a *reed*—a metal or wood slat usually located in the mouthpiece of the instrument—to produce vibrations, which we hear as sounds. Most woodwind instruments also have holes that the player fingers to control pitch.

With brass instruments, the player controls the sound by either tensing or relaxing his or her lips. Many brass instruments have valves which allow the player to control pitch by opening and closing.

Percussion Instruments. Percussion instruments are usually shaken or hit with the hand or a mallet. Drums, cymbals, tambourines, and gongs are examples of percussion instruments.

Keyboard Instruments. Keyboard instruments are played by pressing keys that either control hammers that hit strings, as in pianos, or open and close tubes, as in pipe organs.

Vibration. All sound is vibration. When an object vibrates, it sets the air around it in motion, which causes sound waves. We hear these waves as sounds—as music, as a dog barking, as a whisper, and so on.

THE CHALLENGE

Now that you've learned about instruments and sound, it's time to invent a musical instrument of your own. You can use any or all of the materials in this kit, as well as any household tools and materials that you may have collected.

The musical instrument must be able to make music. How it makes musical sounds, and how many different types of musical sounds it makes, is up to you.

⚙ STEP ONE: BRAINSTORM

List, sketch, and discuss your ideas for a musical instrument. Don't limit yourself to just a few ideas and don't force yourself to think of too many. When you have listed all of your ideas, move on.

⚙ STEP TWO: ASK QUESTIONS AND THINK INVENTIVELY

Questions and Ideas for Creative Thinking:

Can you think of a way to combine different types of instruments to make a new class of instrument? For example, can you combine a string instrument with a percussion instrument to create the percusso–string class?

What would you add to your instrument? What would change about your instrument?

List as many combinations of instrument classes as you can.

Can you think of a musical instrument invention that combines parts of classes of instruments? What would you call it?

Questions and Ideas for Critical Thinking:

How will you play your musical instrument? Will you be able to teach others how to play it?

Will you use the traditional system of musical notation or will you come up with a new system?

Will you be able to play familiar music with your instrument?

✿ STEP THREE: INVENT IT!

You're ready to start inventing. Use everything that you've learned, and as you probably know by now, there's no one correct answer. Keep trying even if your first invention doesn't work. And you can always go back to the "Thinking Tools" section and Step Two to figure out where you went wrong.

If you get stuck and need a hint, turn to "If You Get Stuck" on page 65. And if you really need help, look at the solution in the same section for one possible inventive answer.

Invention Challenge #5:
Invent a Gear-driven Telescoping Machine

A lever is a tool used to multiply force and is the basic element of a telescoping machine.

A lever is usually a rod shaft or arm and is composed of the fulcrum, the effort, and the load. The fulcrum is the fixed point upon which the lever sits, or around which it rotates. The effort is the force applied to do the work. The load is the object you are trying to move and the resistance you are trying to overcome.

No one knows when levers were first used, but we do know that pre-historic people used them for very simple lifting tasks. They used levers to extract water from shallow wells, to move and lift heavy objects, and as balances for weighing things. The ancient Greeks used levers to make weapons (the catapult) and to make wine (the wine press).

Today, levers are used everywhere. They are so common that we often overlook them. We even have levers in our bodies—our arms can be thought of as levers. The elbow is the fulcrum, and the muscles provide the work (the effort) to lift an object (the load) in the hand.

The position of the fulcrum is crucial to how a lever works. Generally, the closer the fulcrum is to the load, the less effort is needed to move the load. Levers are classified into three types according to the positions of the fulcrum, load, and effort.

First-Class Levers. In a first-class lever, the fulcrum is located somewhere between the load and the effort. If the fulcrum is located exactly in the center, the lever is called a balance, because an effort and load of equal weight will keep the lever perfectly balanced. Thus, a balance makes a good weighing tool. Other examples of first-class levers are handcarts, or the nail-extractor ends of hammers.

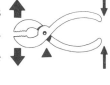

A compound first-class lever is a pair of levers attached or hinged at the fulcrum, which would be located somewhere between the load and effort. Examples are scissors and pliers.

Second-Class Levers. In a second-class lever, the fulcrum is located at one end of the lever. Examples are a wheelbarrow and a bottlecap opener. Effort is applied at the end of the lever opposite the fulcrum—the load is in between. Second-class levers are good for lifting and pressing things.

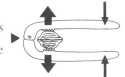

A compound second-class lever is a pair of levers attached or hinged at the fulcrum, which would be located near the load. An example is a nutcracker.

Third-Class Levers. In a third-class lever, the fulcrum is at one end just as in a second-class lever, but the load, not the effort, is at the opposite end. The effort is applied between the two—usually an upward-lifting motion instead of a downward-pressing motion. Examples of third-class levers are a hammer and a fishing rod.

A compound third-class lever is a pair of levers attached or hinged at the fulcrum, which would be located near the effort. An example is a pair of tweezers.

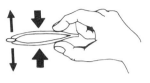

THE CHALLENGE

You've learned a few of the main principles of levers, so it's time to invent a gear-driven telescoping device that uses them. Use any or all of the materials in this kit, as well as any household tools and materials that you may have collected.

The device must extend your reach using levers and gears. How it extends it, and how far it extends it, is up to you.

⚙ STEP ONE: BRAINSTORM

List, sketch, and discuss your ideas for your invention. Don't limit yourself to just a few ideas and don't force them either. When you have listed all of your ideas, move on.

⚙ STEP TWO: ASK QUESTIONS AND THINK INVENTIVELY
Questions and Ideas for Creative Thinking:

What materials in your kit can act as levers?

Will you use simple or compound levers for your reaching device?

Which class of levers will you use? Will you combine different classes?

How will you connect the levers to gears?

Questions and Ideas for Critical Thinking:

What materials will you use?

What are the advantages and disadvantages of your design?

Can you think of a way to make your telescoping device move objects? Could you use it to raise or lower objects?

⚙ STEP THREE: INVENT IT!

Use everything that you've learned and start inventing. Keep at it—there's no correct answer—and even if your first invention doesn't work, you can always go back to the "Thinking Tools" section and Step Two to figure out where you went wrong.

If you get stuck and need a hint, turn to "If You Get Stuck" on page 65. And if you really need help, look at the solution in the same section for one possible inventive answer.

PART FOUR

IF YOU GET STUCK

HINTS

If you're stuck, but you don't want to turn to one possible solution yet, you might find these hints helpful. Don't give up—the best inventions don't come to mind right away. Inventors often struggle many times before perfecting their devices.

So read on, and take these hints as you need them. And remember that the hints and solutions only guide you to one of many different possibilities—you can use them to find your own path!

HINTS FOR INVENTING A
TIME TRACKER

Think about ways to use the rising and falling water level in a water clock as a part of your time tracker. What if you floated something on the water? What if this floating object were somehow attached to another object? As the water level changed, the floating object would rise or fall with the water.

If the floating object had a string attached to it, could it move something attached to the other end of the string? Could the movement of an object at the other end be used to track time?

HINTS FOR INVENTING A
FLYING MACHINE

The source of power for a paper airplane is your arm. What else could you use for a power source on a paper airplane? Remember, a paper airplane doesn't weigh much, so the power source shouldn't weigh much either.

How could you use air to power a paper airplane? And, while you're thinking about this, don't forget to consider Newton's law of equal and opposite reactions!

HINTS FOR INVENTING A
SELF-PROPELLED VEHICLE

Experiment with the electric motor for a self-propelled vehicle invention. Think about how you can connect the spinning shaft of the motor to an axle on the car. Can you think of a way to use a rubber band? Will the vehicle have front-wheel or rear-wheel drive?

The motor needs to be connected to either the front or rear axle. Think about this as you design the vehicle. How will you turn the car on and off? Can you make a switch?

HINTS FOR INVENTING A
MUSICAL THINGAMAGIG

People make instruments all the time. Drumming your fingers on a desk, tapping with a pencil, stretching or plucking a rubber band or string are all examples of how we naturally create "instruments" with which we make musical sounds.

Think about these common, almost unconscious, approaches to musical instrument making and take it from there. How many things can you make that will produce an interesting sound when tapped, plucked, or rattled? Think of ways to make things vibrate.

HINTS FOR INVENTING A
GEAR-DRIVEN TELESCOPING MACHINE

Experiment with ways to combine the gears and a series of compound levers. How could the rotation of gears move a telescoping device that you make out of craft sticks?

Think about what happens when you roll down or roll up the window of a car. Circular motion is changed to vertical motion. Can you think of a way to do this using gears and the craft sticks?

SOLUTIONS

INVENTING A TIME TRACKER:
A WATER-DIAL CLOCK

Remember the water clock discussed on pages 42–43? Well, that's what you're going to invent.

What you need: a 16-ounce or 1-liter plastic soda bottle and cap; a strong card-board box, about 16 inches high; one wooden dowel; two corks; five pieces of string (each one long enough to reach diagonally across the top of the box); a wooden spool; some clay; the plastic pointer; a hammer and nail; a small pan or dish

Instructions:

1. Cut off the bottom of the plastic bottle so that you have the top and

about 4" of bottle bottom. Take off the cap and make a small hole in the center of the cap with a hammer and nail. Now screw the cap back on tightly.

   Make four evenly-spaced holes around the newly-cut edge of the bottle. Space the holes like the four directions of a compass.

   Tie a piece of string to each hole.

2. Now make holes in each corner of the box. Suspend the plastic bottle—cap-side down—inside the box by tying one string from each corner of the bottle to each hole in the corners of the box.

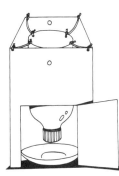

3. Cut a "door" in the back of the box that is big enough to place a pan or a dish under the plastic bottle. This will collect the water as it drips out.

4. Punch or cut two small holes for the dowel, straight through the front and the back of the box and above the bottle. Make sure that the holes line up so that the dowel will be right above the plastic bottle and can turn easily. Don't worry if you misjudge the holes at first—just pick a new spot and try again.

5. With a nail or pencil, carve a hole through the top of one cork. Now slip the cork onto the dowel, inside the box. Push the dowel end out the back hole. The cork should be in the middle of the box, above the bottle.

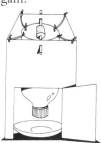

6. Now cut a blank clock face out of paper and place the center of the face through the end of the dowel outside the box. Tape the pointer from the kit onto the end of this dowel, so that the pointer is on top of the clock face but not touching it.

7. Take the fifth piece of string. Tie one end around the wooden spool and the other end around the remaining cork. Place some clay on the end with the dangling cork for a weight.

There should be about 5 inches of string be-tween the spool and the cork.

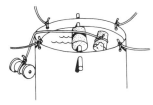8. Drape the string over the cork on the dowel. The tied, weighted cork should be inside the bottle, and the spool should dangle outside.

9. Pour some water into the plastic bottle. The cork should float on the waterline. If it sinks, remove clay until it floats.

If water goes out too fast, drop a thumbtack or a big-headed pin into the plastic bottle, or push a thin piece of paper or clay into the hole to plug it up a little bit. If the water flows too slowly, punch another small hole in the bottlecap. You want the water to flow slowly, but not too slowly.

10. As the water empties out of the bottle, the clay-weighted cork slowly drops, pulling on the string, which turns the dowel. The clock hand attached to the dowel should move, and this movement can be measured. This is how you track time!

11. On the face of the clock, turn the pointer to the top and mark that spot as your starting point. Time your clock for two or three minutes. Mark where the hand points at the end.

Refill your clock. Predict and test where the one-minute mark is. What about five minutes?

In this way, you can make a clock face with minute marks to track time.

12. When you've got the timing figured out, sit back, relax, and watch the clock—you've invented a time tracker!

INVENTING A FLYING MACHINE:
A BALLOON-POWERED STUNT JET

What you need: a few sheets of 8 1/2" x 11" paper; a straw; a paper clip or brass fastener; a dowel; tape; a balloon

Instructions:

1. Fold a piece of paper into an airplane—take a sheet and fold it in half the long way. Fold down two corners into triangles that meet in the middle.

Now fold these triangles over two more times, each time meeting in the middle. Fold the triangles back over themselves to the edge of the paper to make wings.

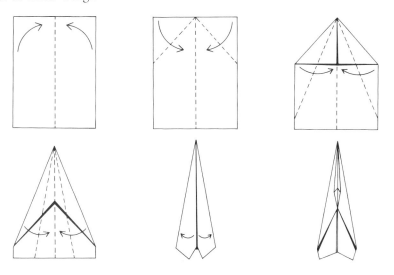

2. Tape a paper clip or a brass fastener to the nose of the jet for weight.

3. Place a straw along the outside bottom of the jet and tape it into place. Make sure that the straw goes along the bottom, not the side, of the jet.

4. Blow up a balloon and temporarily close it with a paper clip—or just hold it closed.

5. Center the jet on top of the balloon so that the nose of the jet points away from the balloon opening. Carefully tape the jet along the balloon. Make sure that it is centered and that it points in a straight line away from the balloon's opening.

6. Use the dowel as a launch guide for the jet. Stick it into a base—clay or cardboard, tape it to a book, or ask a friend to hold it for you. It should be positioned at a slight angle.

Insert the dowel into the back of the jet straw and release the balloon. The force of the air escaping from the balloon will propel your jet!

7. Experiment with different materials and papers to see what flies fastest, longest, and straightest!

INVENTING A SELF-PROPELLED VEHICLE:
A TRIANGULAR RACE CAR

What you need: four spools; two dowels; three splints (two triple drilled, one double drilled); four rubber bands; two brass fasteners; a battery-powered motor; an AA battery; tape; two paper clips

Instructions:

1. Take one three-holed splint and slide a dowel through one of the end holes. Place three spools on the dowel.

Now put the dowel through one of the end holes of another three-holed splint.

The spools should be in between the splints.

2. Place a rubber band around the remaining spool. Slide the spool and rubber band onto the other dowel.

Form a triangle by putting the dowel through the opposite end-holes of the splints. The single spool with the rubber band around it should also be in between the splints, across from the other three spools.

3. Fasten the motor to the remaining wood splint with a rubber band. Place the motor splint (or shaft) across the other wood splints.

Secure brass fasteners in the middle holes of the wooden splints. These splints will act as the frame of the car.

Stretch a rubber band from each fastener over the shaft in the motor splint and back around the ends of the three-spool dowel.

They will hold the motor splint to the triangle.

4. Lay the battery across the motor shaft so that it is out of the way and attach it to the car using tape or rubber bands.

Connect the motor wires to the battery with tape. The motor will turn on immediately.

To create a switch, keep both wires taped to the battery, and cut the wires in the middle. The motor will stop. Attach both ends of the cut wires to paper clips. Clip the wired clips to a section of the splint, but do not let them touch.

When you want to turn the car on, slide one paper clip over so that it touches the other one!

5. The rubber band on the single spool is the drive belt. Place this rubber band around the spinning shaft of the motor. The vehicle will go forward or backward—depending on which way you twist the rubber band. Experiment to find out which way works best.

6. Congratulate yourself—you've invented a triangular race car! Experiment with your invention. What can you add to make it go faster? Will the propeller help?

INVENTING A MUSICAL THINGAMAGIG:
A PERCUSSO-STRING INSTRUMENT

What you need: two dowels; ten rubber bands; a bell; a sheet of paper or plastic wrap; a pencil; an empty cardboard box less than 6" in width; two toilet paper tubes; two marbles; three brass fasteners; two triple-drilled splints; a spool

Instructions:

1. Make a drum by stretching plastic wrap or paper over one end of a toilet paper tube. This makes a drum skin. Secure the skin in place with a rubber band. Make another drum, but this time, cover both ends with drum skin after putting the two marbles in the tube.

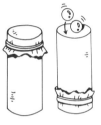

2. Along one of the long sides of the box, cut two holes the size of the toilet paper tubes and insert the drums.

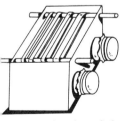

3. To make stretched strings for playing, collect several rubber bands of various lengths and widths. Punch holes along each long side of the box.

Insert one dowel through a side of the box and run the dowel inside one end of each rubber band before inserting the dowel through the other side of the box.

Insert the second dowel through one side of the box and stretch the rubber bands around it before inserting it through the other side.

4. Use the splints and bell to make a bell flicker. Place the center hole of a

triple-drilled splint over the top of one of the dowels. Stack a spool and another triple-drilled splint on top.

Wrap tape around the top of the dowel to hold these pieces in place. Now, wrap a rubber band around the head of a brass fastener and insert them both through one end-hole of the top splint.

Bend the brass fastener legs to anchor the rubber band. Stretch the rubber band across to the bottom splint hole and anchor it there with a brass fastener. The rubber band should be stretched tightly between the dowels.

Attach the bell to the other end of the top splint with a rubber band or tape. Attach the bell flicker to the box with tape.

5. Wrap a ball of plastic wrap around the eraser end of a pencil and secure it with a rubber band.

Use this as a mallet to hit the drums, the sides of the box, or even the bell.

Flick the bell by plucking the rubber band end of the bell flicker. Strum the rubber bands inside the box to make music and keep the beat with your percussion instruments.

6. Make up music, songs, and play on!

INVENTING A GEAR-DRIVEN TELESCOPING MACHINE: AN AUTOMATIC TELESCOPER

What you need: four two-holed splints; two three-holed splints; seven brass fasteners; the large gear; the small gear; the gear handle; a spool; glue; masking tape; a sturdy cardboard box (about 10" x 13")

Instructions:

1. Begin by making telescoping levers. Cross two double-drilled splints to form an "X." Insert a brass fastener through the center holes to connect them.

Use brass fasteners to attach the ends of two triple-drilled splints to the "X."

Cross the newly-attached triple-drilled splints and connect their centers with another fastener.

Attach the remaining double-drilled splints with fasteners to the ends of the triple-drilled X that you just made. Now cross them and connect their centers with the last fastener.

Practice extending and retracting the telescoping levers. Hold them at one end and slowly move the splints together to make the arms extend. Move the splints apart to make the arms retract.

2. Now you need to set up a gear system which will automatically open and close the telescoping levers.

You'll need a sturdy piece of cardboard that sits slightly off the ground. The lid from a shirt box works well, as does a gift box.

Position the large and small gears in the bottom right corner of the cardboard. (Note: position the gears as close to the right edge as possible.)

Place the large gear with the flat side down and mark its position by pushing a straightened paper clip through the center hole.

Carefully push a sharpened pencil through the mark to make a hole in the box.

Now, insert the gear stem through the hole. Lay the small gear to the left of the large gear so that the teeth fit together. Repeat the steps above to make a hole for the small gear.

3. To control the range of the motion, you'll need to make a "track" in the box. Place a ruler across the center of the gear-holes and draw a line that extends to the edge of the box, left of the gears.

Starting 1/2" from the left edge of the box, cut out a rectangle 5" long and 1/2" wide. The line you drew is the bottom edge of the rectangle.

4. Position the telescoping levers so that the brass fastener *heads* are facing up.

Glue the spool to the end of the splint on the right side. Then pick up the small gear and glue the flat face of the small gear to the end of the splint on the left.

Make sure that the teeth of the gear extend beyond the edge of the splint.

5. Position the telescoping levers on the cardboard with the brass fastener heads facing down. Insert the small gear into its hole and insert the spool onto the rectangle track.

You can wrap tape or a very small rubber band around the back of each gear (inside the box) so that they don't pop out.

6. Place the gear handle into the large gearhole.

Turn the large gear. As it rotates, it turns the small gear, which moves the telescoping levers out!

The spool moves back and forth in the track, controlling the range of motion. This device is similar to the mechanics of a car window.

7. Attach the ends of the telescoper to a puppet or another object to raise and lower it. You might even attach it to a light window shade to open and close it!

YOUNG INVENTOR PROFILE

Kindergartner Katie Harding invented the Mudpuddle Spotter. This umbrella with a flashlight attached to the handle makes it easier to avoid puddles when walking in the rain after dark.

WHERE CAN I GO FROM HERE?

PART FIVE

A Quick Guide to Patents: Protecting Your Ideas

As you explore your ideas and inventive skills, you may come up with an invention that you want to tell people about, and even manufacture! Before you do this, you might want to apply for a legal document that proves you own your invention.

A patent helps to protect your invention. It lets everyone know that your invention belongs to you and that no one can use, make, or sell it without your permission.

To be eligible for a patent, you need to be able to answer "yes" to three questions: Is your invention new? Is your invention useful? Does your invention work?

You also need to be able to prove that you were the first person to think of the idea. It's possible that someone living somewhere else invented the same thing you did. To prove you thought of it first, you need to be able to provide the date you first came up with the idea.

How Do I Apply for a Patent? If you think your invention meets all the requirements, the next step is to apply for a patent. The process is very complicated, so you might want to ask an adult to help you.

You'll need a written description and a drawing of your invention. Both of these should include enough detail so that anyone could make a model from your description.

A patent examiner at the Office of Patent and Trademark will then review your application and search the patent files to see whether your invention has already been patented. This process can take an average of two years to complete and can cost a lot of money.

If you decide not to get a patent, you can try a "postage stamp patent," a trick inventors often use to prove when they came up with their ideas. All you have to do is write a description of your invention and draw a sketch of it. Sign and date the paper in front of a friend, who acts as a witness. Your friend needs to sign his or her name, too.

Seal the paper in an envelope, address it to yourself, and send the envelope to yourself via registered mail. When it comes back to you, don't open it—keep it sealed and store it in a safe place.

If anyone questions when you thought of your invention, the letter and postmark date will be your proof. This kind of patent does not usually have any legal value, but it can help you prove to your friends that your invention was your idea.

To find out more about patents, you can obtain a free brochure called "Basic Facts About Patents" by writing to:

Office of Patent and Trademark
Washington, DC 20231

Conclusion: Inventiveness Isn't Just for Inventing Anymore

Now that you've learned to recognize and tap into your inventive spirit, you need to work on preserving it. Inventors aren't just inventive when they're in their workshops—they're inventive in everyday life, too!

Whether you're inventing a toy car, a faster method for cleaning your room, or even a clever way to end an argument between friends, you're using the same inventive spirit.

That spirit is based on remembering that there are different ways of looking at things. This kit can help you recognize the many uses of common items. And you have experienced first hand the many different ways to make things like clocks, toy cars, musical instruments, and flying machines.

Now, you can be the one that people turn to when they need to figure things out, whether it's fixing a leaky faucet, inventing a new game, or writing an essay! And chances are, you'll be a happier person because you can see things in many different ways.

INVENTOR'S WORKBOOK

The pages from here to the end of the book have been left blank for your inventing. Use them to brainstorm, sketch, organize, and rethink your ideas.

ABOUT THE AUTHOR

Belinda Recio works at the Museum of Science in Boston, where she manages "one big Inventor's Workshop"—the product development program. She is also a freelance writer who has published articles on topics from kaleidoscopes to printmaking and herbs. She earned her M.A. in English at Southern Connecticut University.